Sc.R.E.A.M

Science Rules Everything Around Me

Penmanship Practice for the Scientist in You

Pamela R. C. Robinson

Dedication

My village, extensive in number, brilliance, & wisdom. I am
nothing without you & God.
Your favorite scientist & AP,
PamJr

Acknowledgements

God, thank you for your patience.
Mommy, thank you for your unwavering support.
Toodah, thank you for showing us the world through your eyes. American Publisher, Inc, buckle up, we have more creating to do.

About the Author

A 10+ year educator that has taught 6th – 8th grade science, Biomedical science, Biology, AP Biology, Chemistry, Physics, Physical Science, & Health… it's safe to say that PamJr LOVES science. Through her tenure she noticed a sharp decline in student ability to spell & write legibly, thus, the Sc.R.E.A.M. series was born, designed to infuse letters, numbers, words, sentences, & yep, you guessed it, SCIENCE.

About the Periodic Table of Elements

The Periodic Table of Elements was first developed by Russian chemist Dmitry Mendeleyev in 1869. Most commonly introduced in Chemistry, the Periodic Table of Elements is a collection of all the chemical elements organized by increasing **atomic number**. The elements with similar properties are found in the same **column** or **groups** and elements with the same number of occupied **electron shells** are found in the same **rows** or **periods**. Elements are also grouped in the following categories:

1. Metals
   a. There are so many metals that they are further divided into the following:
      i. Alkali Metals
      ii. Alkaline Earth Metals
      iii. Transition Metals
      iv. Basic Metals
      v. Lanthanides (Rare Earth)
      vi. Actinides (Radioactive)
2. Metalloids
3. Nonmetals
   a. These are divided into the following:
      i. Nonmetals
      ii. Halogens
      iii. Noble Gases

P.S.
As you work through this book you will come across words & concepts that you are not familiar with, **THAT IS OK**! Grab your parent, guardian, or trusted adult and conduct your OWN research to stretch your brain. The world of science is MASSIVE and it's all right at your fingertips.

Happy exploring,
Ms. Pam, Jr.
Your favorite scientist & Assistant Principal

Table of Contents

<u>Hydrogen</u> makes up over 90% of all the atoms in the universe.

Name:_______________________________________ Date: _____________________________

Name:__________________________________ Date: ______________________

The atomic symbol for

Hydrogen is H.

Name:_________________________________ Date: _____________________

The atomic number for

Hydrogen is one.

Name:_________________________________ Date: ____________________

The atomic mass for Hydrogen

is 1.008.

____
Atomic Number

____
Element symbol

____
Element Name

____
Atomic Mass

At room temperature, <u>Helium</u> is an odorless, tasteless, colorless gas.

Name:____ Date: __________________________

Helium   Helium   Helium   Helium

Name:____ Date: _____________________

The atomic symbol for Helium

is He.

The atomic number for Helium is two.

Name:______________________________________ Date: ____________________

The atomic mass for Helium is

4.003.

____

Atomic Number

____

Element symbol

____

Element Name

____

Atomic Mass

<u>Lithium</u> is the lightest metal.

Name:_______________________________________ Date: _______________________

Lithium Lithium Lithium Lithium

Name:__________________________________ Date: ___________________

The atomic symbol for Lithium

is Li.

Name:_______________________________________ Date: _________________________

The atomic number for Lithium

is three.

The atomic mass for Lithium is
is 6.941.

FILL IN THE BLANKS BELOW WITH THE CORRECT INFORMATION

15

____

Atomic Number

____

Element symbol

____

Element Name

____

Atomic Mass

<u>Beryllium</u> is non-magnetic.

Name:_________________________________ Date: _______________________

Beryllium   Beryllium   Beryllium

Beryllium

Name:____ Date: _____________________

The atomic symbol for

Beryllium is Be.

The atomic number for

Beryllium is four.

The atomic mass for Berylium

is 9.012.

____

Atomic Number

____

Element symbol

____

Element Name

____

Atomic Mass

<u>Boron</u> in its crystalline form is very unreactive.

Name:_______________________________________ Date: ____________________________

Boron   Boron   Boron   Boron

Name:________________________________ Date: ___________________

The atomic symbol for Boron

is B.

Name:____________________________________ Date: ____________________

The atomic number for Boron

is five.

Name:_______________________________________ Date: ___________________________

The atomic mass for Boron is

10.811.

____

Atomic Number

____

Element symbol

____

Element Name

____

Atomic Mass

<u>Carbon</u> is one of the most abundant elements in the universe.

Name:____ Date: _____________________

Carbon Carbon Carbon Carbon

Name:_________________________________ Date:____________________

The atomic symbol for Carbon

is C.

Name:____ Date: ___________________________

The atomic number for Carbon

is six.

Name:____ Date: _____________________

The atomic mass for Carbon is

12.011.

____

Atomic Number

____

Element symbol

____

Element Name

____

Atomic Mass

<u>Nitrogen</u> makes up more than half of the atmosphere's gas.

Name:_________________________________ Date:_________________________

Nitrogen   Nitrogen   Nitrogen

Nitrogen

The atomic symbol for

Nitrogen is N.

The atomic number for

Nitrogen is seven.

The atomic mass for Nitrogen

is 14.007.

35

____

Atomic Number

____

Element symbol

____

Element Name

____

Atomic Mass

Name:_________________________________   Date: _________________________

Oxygen   Oxygen   Oxygen

Oxygen

Name:____ Date: _____________________

The atomic symbol for Oxygen

is O.

Name:____ Date: _____________________

The atomic number for Oxygen
is eight.

The atomic mass for Oxygen is 15.999.

____

Atomic Number

____

Element symbol

____

Element Name

____

Atomic Mass

Fluorine is the most reactive & most electronegative of all chemical elements.

Name:_______________________________________ Date: _____________________________

Fluorine   Fluorine   Fluorine

Fluorine

Name:_____________________________________ Date: _____________________

The atomic symbol for Fluorine
is F.

The atomic number for Fluorine is nine.

Name:_________________________________ Date: _______________________

The atomic mass for Fluorine is

18.998.

____
Atomic Number

____
Element symbol

____
Element Name

____
Atomic Mass

<u>Neon</u> is found in the stars.

Name:____ Date: _______________________

Neon Neon Neon Neon

The atomic symbol for Neon is

Ne.

Name:_________________________________ Date: _____________________

Name:_______________________________ Date: _______________________

The atomic mass for Neon is

20.180.

FILL IN THE BLANKS BELOW WITH THE CORRECT INFORMATION

50

____

Atomic Number

____

Element symbol

____

Element Name

____

Atomic Mass

At room temperature, <u>Sodium</u> metal is soft enough to cut with a butter knife.

Name:_______________________________________ Date: _______________________

Name:____ Date:___________________________

Name:____ Date: _____________________

The atomic number for Sodium
is eleven.

Name:_________________________________ Date: ___________________

The atomic mass for Sodium is
is 22.990.

55

____

Atomic Number

Element symbol

Element Name

Atomic Mass

<u>**Magnesium**</u> **is the most lightweight out of all the metallic elements.**

Name:_______________________________________   Date: _______________________

Magnesium   Magnesium

Magnesium   Magnesium

Name:________________________________ Date:_________________________

The atomic symbol for

Magnesium is Mg.

Name:________________________________ Date: ____________________

The atomic number for

Magnesium is twelve.

Name:_______________________________________ Date: _____________________________

The atomic mass for

Magnesium is 24.305.

____
Atomic Number

____
Element symbol

____
Element Name

____
Atomic Mass

<u>Aluminum</u> is very ductile, & it may be shaped into a lot of things.

Name:____ Date:_____________________

Aluminum Aluminum Aluminum

Aluminum

The atomic symbol for

Aluminum is Al.

The atomic number for

Aluminum is thirteen.

The atomic mass for Aluminum is 26.982.

65

____

Atomic Number

____

Element symbol

____

Element Name

____

Atomic Mass

<u>Silicon</u> is a naturally occurring element not to be confused with silicone.

Name:____ Date: _____________________

Silicon   Silicon   Silicon   Silicon

Name:___________________________________ Date: ___________________________

The atomic symbol for Silicon

is Si.

The atomic number for Silicon is fourteen.

Name:_________________________________ Date: _________________________

The atomic mass for Silicon is

28.086.

Atomic Number

Element symbol

Element Name

Atomic Mass

<u>Phosphorus</u> is a solid at room temperature.

Name:_________________________________   Date:____________________

Name:____ Date: _____________________

The atomic symbol for

Phosphorus is P.

Name:____ Date: _____________________

The atomic number for

Phosphorus is fifteen.

The atomic mass for

Phosphorus is 30.974.

75

____

Atomic Number

____

Element symbol

____

Element Name

____

Atomic Mass

Although many <u>Sulfur</u> compounds have a strong smell, the
pure element is odorless.

Name: _______________________________________ Date: _____________________

Sulfur   Sulfur   Sulfur   Sulfur

Name:____ Date: _____________________

The atomic symbol for Sulfur is

S

The atomic number for Sulfur is sixteen.

Name:_________________________________ Date: _____________________

The atomic mass for Sulfur is

32.065.

____
Atomic Number

____
Element symbol

____
Element Name

____
Atomic Mass

<u>Chlorine</u> gas appears to be yellow-green in color.

Name:_______________________________________ Date: _____________________________

Chlorine   Chlorine   Chlorine

Chlorine

Name:________________________________ Date: ____________________

The atomic symbol for Chlorine

is Cl.

The atomic number for Chlorine is seventeen.

The atomic mass for Chlorine is 35.453.

85

____

Atomic Number

____

Element symbol

____

Element Name

____

Atomic Mass

<u>Argon</u> is the most abundant noble gas.

Name:______________________________________ Date: ______________________

Argon   Argon   Argon   Argon

Name:_________________________________ Date: _____________________

The atomic symbol for Argon is

Ar.

The atomic number for Argon is eighteen.

Name:____ Date: _____________________

The atomic mass for Argon is

39.948

90

____
Atomic Number

____
Element symbol

____
Element Name

____
Atomic Mass

<u>Potassium</u> burn with a bright red in a flame test.

Name:_______________________________________ Date: _____________________

Potassium   Potassium

Potassium   Potassium

Name:_______________________________________ Date: _____________________

The atomic symbol for

Potassium is K.

Name:_______________________________________ Date: _______________________

The atomic number for

Potassium is nineteen.

Name:____ Date: _________________________

The atomic mass for Potassium
is 39.098.

95

____

Atomic Number

____

Element symbol

____

Element Name

____

Atomic Mass

<u>Calcium</u> comes from the Latin word "calcis/calx" meaning "lime."

Name:____ Date: ____________________

The atomic symbol for Calcium

is Ca.

Name:____ Date: ____________________

The atomic number for Calcium

is twenty.

Name:_________________________________ Date: _______________________

The atomic mass for Calcium is

40.078.

____

Atomic Number

____

Element symbol

____

Element Name

____

Atomic Mass

When exposed to air, pure <u>Scandium</u> develops a pink-yellow oxidation layer.

Name:____ Date: ____________________________

Scandium Scandium Scandium

Scandium

The atomic symbol for

Scandium is Sc.

Name:_________________________________ Date: _________________________

The atomic number for

Scandium is twenty-one.

Name:_________________________________ Date: ___________________

The atomic mass for Scandium
is 44.956.

____

Atomic Number

____

Element symbol

____

Element Name

____

Atomic Mass

<u>Titanium</u> is naturally resistant to corrosion.

Name:____ Date: ________________________

Titanium   Titanium   Titanium

Titanium

Name:_________________________________ Date:_______________________

The atomic symbol for

Titanium is Ti.

Name:_________________________________ Date: _________________________

The atomic number for

Titanium is twenty two.

Name:____ Date:____________________

The atomic mass for Titanium

is 47.867.

____

Atomic Number

____

Element symbol

____

Element Name

____

Atomic Mass

Most of the world's <u>Vanadium</u> comes from China, Russia, or South Africa.

Name:_______________________________________   Date:______________________

Vanadium   Vanadium

Vanadium   Vanadium

Name:_______________________________________ Date: ___________________

The atomic symbol for

Vanadium is V.

Name:________________________________ Date: ________________

The atomic number for

Vanadium is twenty-three.

Name:_________________________________ Date: _________________________

The atomic mass for Vanadium

is 50.942.

____

Atomic Number

____

Element symbol

____

Element Name

____

Atomic Mass

<u>Chromium</u> has natural anti-rusting properties.

Name:_________________________________ Date: _______________________

Chromium   Chromium

Chromium   Chromium

Name:____ Date: ____________________

The atomic symbol for

Chromium is Cr.

Name:_______________________________________ Date: _______________________

The atomic number for

Chromium is twenty four.

The atomic mass for Chromium is 51.996.

FILL IN THE BLANKS BELOW WITH THE CORRECT INFORMATION

Atomic Number

Element symbol

Element Name

Atomic Mass

During WWII, <u>Manganese</u> replaced most of the Nickel in US coins,
when nickel became scarce.

Name:________________________________   Date: ___________________

Manganese   Manganese

Manganese   Manganese

Name:_____________________________________ Date: _____________________

The atomic symbol for

Manganese is Mn.

Name:_________________________________ Date:_______________________

The atomic number for

Manganese is twenty five.

Name:_______________________________ Date: _______________________

The atomic mass for

Manganese is 54.938.

125

____

Atomic Number

____

Element symbol

____

Element Name

____

Atomic Mass

<u>**Iron's**</u> **scientific name is Ferrum.**

Name:____ Date: ________________________

Iron　　Iron　　Iron　　Iron

Name:____ Date: _____________________

The atomic symbol for Iron is

Fe.

The atomic number for Iron is twenty six.

Name:____ Date:_____________________________

The atomic mass for Iron is

55.845

____

Atomic Number

____

Element symbol

____

Element Name

____

Atomic Mass

<u>Cobalt</u> is a hard, brittle metal with a bluish-white color.

Name:____ Date:_____________________________

Cobalt Cobalt Cobalt Cobalt

Name:_________________________________ Date:_______________________

The atomic symbol for Cobalt is Co.

Name:____ Date:___________________________

The atomic number for Cobalt

is twenty seven.

Name:_________________________________ Date: _________________________

The atomic mass for Cobalt is
58.933.

135

____
Atomic Number

____
Element symbol

____
Element Name

____
Atomic Mass

<u>Nickel</u> is found in stainless steel, magnets, coins & batteries.

Name:_________________________________ Date: _______________________

Nickel   Nickel   Nickel   Nickel

Name:______________________________________   Date: ____________________

The atomic symbol for Nickle is

Ni.

137

Name:____ Date: _____________________

The atomic number for Nickle is twenty eight.

Name:____ Date:_____________________

The atomic mass for Nickle is

58.693.

____

Atomic Number

____

Element symbol

____

Element Name

____

Atomic Mass

<u>Copper</u> is an excellent conductor of heat & electricity.

Name:____ Date:_______________________________

Copper Copper Copper Copper

Name:____ Date:____________________________

The atomic symbol for Copper
is Cu.

Name:_________________________________ Date:___________________

The atomic number for Copper

is twenty nine.

Name:_______________________________________ Date: _____________________

The atomic mass for Copper is
is 63.546.

145

____

Atomic Number

____

Element symbol

____

Element Name

____

Atomic Mass

<u>Zinc</u> is essential for the growth & development of almost all lives.

Name:____ Date: _____________________

Zinc   Zinc   Zinc   Zinc

The atomic symbol for Zinc is

Zn.

Name:_______________________________________ Date: _____________________

The atomic number for Zinc is

thirty.

Name:____ Date:_____________________________

The atomic mass for Zinc is

65.390.

FILL IN THE BLANKS BELOW WITH THE CORRECT INFORMATION

____

Atomic Number

____

Element symbol

____

Element Name

____

Atomic Mass

When painted on glass, <u>Gallium</u> turns into a lustrous mirror.

Name:____ Date:__________________________

Gallium   Gallium   Gallium

Gallium

Name:_______________________________________ Date: ___________________

The atomic symbol for Gallium
is Ga.

Name:_______________________________________ Date: _______________________

The atomic number for Gallium

is thirty one.

The atomic mass for Gallium is
69.723.

155

____

Atomic Number

____

Element symbol

____

Element Name

____

Atomic Mass

<u>Germanium</u> is mined and produced by China.

Name:_______________________________________ Date: _______________________

Name:_______________________________________ Date: ____________________

The atomic symbol for

Germanium is Ge.

Name:________________________________ Date: ____________________

The atomic number for

Germanium is thirty two.

The atomic mass for

Germanium is 72.640.

____

Atomic Number

____

Element symbol

____

Element Name

____

Atomic Mass

When <u>Arsenic</u> is heated, it oxidizes & releases an odor similar to garlic.

Name:________________________________   Date:____________________________

Arsenic Arsenic Arsenic Arsenic

Name:____ Date: _____________________

The atomic symbol for Arsenic

is As.

Name:_______________________________________ Date:_____________________________

The atomic number for Arsenic

is thirty three.

Name:_________________________________ Date: ___________________

The atomic mass for Arsenic is

74.922.

____

Atomic Number

____

Element symbol

____

Element Name

____

Atomic Mass

<u>Selenium</u> gets its name from the Greek word "selene," which means "moon."

Name:_________________________________ Date: ___________________

Selenium Selenium Selenium

Selenium

Name:____ Date:_____________________________

The atomic symbol for

Selenium is Se.

Name:_________________________________   Date:_________________________

Name:_______________________________________ Date: _____________________

The atomic mass for Selenium

is 78.960.

____

Atomic Number

____

Element symbol

____

Element Name

____

Atomic Mass

<u>Bromine</u> is liquid at room temperature & has a reddish-brown color in its pure form

Name:_______________________________________   Date:___________________________

Bromine   Bromine   Bromine

Bromine

Name:_______________________________________ Date: _______________________

The atomic symbol for Bromine

is Br.

Name:____ Date: _____________________

The atomic number for Bromine

is thirty five.

The atomic mass for Bromine is
79.904.

____
Atomic Number

____
Element symbol

____
Element Name

____
Atomic Mass

<u>Krypton</u> is a noble gas that is odorless & colorless.

Name: _______________________________________ Date: _____________________

Krypton   Krypton   Krypton

Krypton

The atomic symbol for Krypton

is Kr.

Name:_________________________________ Date: _________________

The atomic number for Krypton

is thirty six.

Name:____ Date: _____________________

The atomic mass for Krypton is

83.800.

____

Atomic Number

____

Element symbol

____

Element Name

____

Atomic Mass

<u>Rubidium</u> can be used to give fireworks a red-violet color.

Name:_________________________________ Date: _______________________

Rubidium Rubidium Rubidium

Rubidium

The atomic symbol for

Rubidium is Rb.

The atomic number for

Rubidium is thirty-seven.

The atomic mass for Rubidium
is 85.468.

185

Atomic Number

Element symbol

Element Name

Atomic Mass

<u>Strontium</u> is a soft metal that has a dull, green, grayish-white appearance.

Name:____ Date: _____________________

Strontium Strontium Strontium

Strontium

Name:______________________________________ Date: ______________________

The atomic symbol for

Strontium is Sr.

Name:____ Date: _____________________

The atomic number for

Strontium is thirty eight.

Name:_________________________________ Date: _______________________

The atomic mass for Strontium

is 87.620.

____

Atomic Number

____

Element symbol

____

Element Name

____

Atomic Mass

<u>Yttrium</u> can be found in the human body in tiny amounts, usually concentrated in the liver, kidneys, & bones.

Name:____ Date: _____________________________

Yttrium Yttrium Yttrium Yttrium

Name:_________________________________ Date: _______________________

Name:____ Date:_____________________________

The atomic number for Yttrium

is thirty nine.

Name:_________________________________ Date: _______________________

The atomic mass for Yttrium is
88.906.

Atomic Number

Element symbol

Element Name

Atomic Mass

The majority of <u>Zirconium</u> comes from Australia or South Africa.

Name:____ Date:____________________________

Zirconium Zirconium Zirconium

Zirconium

Name:____ Date:___________________________

The atomic symbol for

Zirconium is Zr.

The atomic number for

Zirconium is forty.

Name:_______________________________ Date: ________________________

The atomic mass for Zirconium

is 91.224.

____

Atomic Number

____

Element symbol

____

Element Name

____

Atomic Mass

Niobium alloys are frequently used in scientific equipment, especially equipment designed to leave the Earth.

Name:________________________________   Date: _________________________

Niobium   Niobium   Niobium

Niobium

The atomic symbol for Niobium is Nb.

The atomic number for Niobium
is forty one.

Name:____ Date: _______________________

The atomic mass for Niobium is
92.906.

____

Atomic Number

____

Element symbol

____

Element Name

____

Atomic Mass

<u>Molybdenum</u> has one of the highest melting points of all pure elements.

Name:____ Date: _____________________

Molybdenum   Molybdenum

Molybdenum   Molybdenum

The atomic symbol for

Molybdenum is Mo.

Name:_______________________________ Date: _______________________

The atomic number for

Molybdenum is forty two.

Name:______________________________________ Date:______________________

The atomic mass for

Molybdenum is 95.940.

Atomic Number

Element symbol

Element Name

Atomic Mass

<u>Technetium</u> is the only element that is artificially produced.

Name:_______________________________________ Date: _______________________

Technetium   Technetium

Technetium   Technetium

Name:____ Date: _____________________

The atomic symbol for

Technetium is Tc.

Name:____ Date: _____________________

The atomic number for

Technetium is forty three.

The atomic mass for

Technetium is 98.

215

____
Atomic Number

____
Element symbol

____
Element Name

____
Atomic Mass

<u>Ruthenium</u> compounds stain or discolor the skin.

Name:_________________________________ Date: _______________________

Name:_____________________________________ Date: _____________________

The atomic symbol for

Ruthenium is Ru.

The atomic number for Ruthenium is forty four.

Name:______________________________________ Date:___________________________

The atomic mass for

Ruthenium is 101.07.

____

Atomic Number

____

Element symbol

____

Element Name

____

Atomic Mass

<u>Rhodium</u> is an ultra-shiny, corrosion resistant metal.

Name:_________________________________ Date:_______________________

Rhodium   Rhodium   Rhodium

Rhodium

Name:____ Date: _______________________

The atomic symbol for

Rhodium is Rh.

The atomic number for

Rhodium is forty five.

The atomic mass for Rhodium
is 102.906.

____

Atomic Number

____

Element symbol

____

Element Name

____

Atomic Mass

<u>Palladium</u> was discovered in 1803.

Name: _________________________________ Date: _________________________

Palladium Palladium Palladium

Palladium

The atomic symbol for

Palladium is Pd.

Name:____ Date:_________________________

The atomic number for

Palladium is forty six.

The atomic mass for Palladium is 106.420.

230

____

Atomic Number

____

Element symbol

____

Element Name

____

Atomic Mass

<u>Silver</u> is the most reflective metal.

Name:_______________________________________ Date: _______________________

Name:____ Date: _____________________

The atomic symbol for Silver

is Ag.

Name:___________________________________ Date: _____________________

The atomic number for Silver

is forty-seven.

Name:_______________________________________ Date: _____________________

The atomic mass for Silver is

107.868.

235

____
Atomic Number

____
Element symbol

____
Element Name

____
Atomic Mass

<u>Cadmium</u> can be easily cut with a knife.

Name:_________________________________ Date: _______________________

Name:____ Date: ___________________________

The atomic symbol for

Cadmium is Cd.

Name:_______________________________________   Date: _______________________

The atomic number for

Cadmium is forty eight.

The atomic mass for Cadmium

is 112.411.

240

____
Atomic Number

____
Element symbol

____
Element Name

____
Atomic Mass

<u>Indium</u> metal gives off a high-pitched "scream" when bent.

Name:_______________________________________   Date: ______________________

Indium Indium Indium Indium

The atomic symbol for Indium is In.

The atomic number for Indium
is forty-nine.

Name:_________________________________ Date:_______________________

The atomic mass for Indium is

114.818.

245

____
Atomic Number

____
Element symbol

____
Element Name

____
Atomic Mass

<u>Tin</u> makes a screaming sound called a "tin cry" when bent.

Name:____ Date: _______________________

Tin   Tin   Tin   Tin

Name:_________________________________ Date: _________________________

The atomic symbol for Tin is

Sn.

The atomic number for Tin is fifty.

Name:_________________________________ Date: ____________________

The atomic mass for Tin is

118.71.

250

____

Atomic Number

____

Element symbol

____

Element Name

____

Atomic Mass

<u>Antimony</u> is a brittle, bright, shiny, metalloid.

Name:_________________________________   Date: _________________________

Antimony   Antimony   Antimony

Antimony

Name:_________________________________ Date: _______________________

The atomic symbol for

Antimony is Sb.

Name:____ Date: _____________________

The atomic number for

Antimony is fifty-one.

The atomic mass for Antimony is 121.760.

Atomic Number

Element symbol

Element Name

Atomic Mass

<u>Tellurium</u> comes from the Latin word "tells," meaning "Earth."

Name:_____________________________________ Date: ___________________

Tellurium   Tellurium   Tellurium

Tellurium

Name:_____________________________________ Date: _____________________________

The atomic symbol for

Tellurium is Te.

Name:_______________________________________ Date: _______________________

The atomic number for

Tellurium is fifty two.

The atomic mass for Tellurium

is 127.6.

Atomic Number

Element symbol

Element Name

Atomic Mass

<u>Iodine</u> helps regulate our metabolism.

Name:____ Date:______________________

Iodine Iodine Iodine Iodine

The atomic symbol for Iodine is I.

Name:_________________________________ Date: _______________________

The atomic number for Iodine

is fifty three.

The atomic mass for Iodine is 126.905.

____

Atomic Number

____

Element symbol

____

Element Name

____

Atomic Mass

<u>Xenon</u> is a gas primarily used in light manufacturing.

Name:_________________________________ Date: _____________________

Xenon Xenon Xenon Xenon

Name:____________________________________ Date: ____________________

The atomic symbol for Xenon

is Xe.

Name:________________________________ Date: ___________________

The atomic number for Xenon
is fifty four.

Name:_______________________________   Date: _______________________

The atomic mass for Xenon is

131.293.

____

Atomic Number

____

Element symbol

____

Element Name

____

Atomic Mass

<u>Cesium</u> has a boiling point of 1,239.8 °F.

Name:_______________________________________   Date:___________________________

Cesium   Cesium   Cesium

Cesium

The atomic symbol for Cesium is Cs.

Name:____ Date: _____________________

The atomic number for Cesium
is fifty five.

Name:_________________________________ Date: _______________________

The atomic mass for Cesium is

132.906.

275

____
Atomic Number

____
Element symbol

____
Element Name

____
Atomic Mass

<u>Barium</u> was named after the Greek word "bary," meaning "heavy."

Name:_________________________________ Date:_____________________

Barium Barium Barium Barium

Name:_________________________________ Date:_______________________

The atomic symbol for Barium

is Ba.

The atomic number for Barium

is fifty six.

Name:_______________________________________ Date:_____________________

The atomic mass for Barium is

137.327.

____

Atomic Number

____

Element symbol

____

Element Name

____

Atomic Mass

<u>Lanthanum</u> is a metal so soft it can be cut with a butter knife.

Name:_______________________________________ Date: _______________________

The atomic symbol for

Lanthanum is La.

The atomic number for
Lanthanum is fifty seven.

Name:____ Date: ___________________

The atomic mass for

Lanthanum is 138.906.

Atomic Number

Element symbol

Element Name

Atomic Mass

Name:_________________________________ Date: _________________________

Cerium   Cerium   Cerium

Cerium

Name:____ Date: _____________________

The atomic symbol for Cerium

is Ce.

Name:

Name:________________________________ Date: ________________________

The atomic number for Cerium
is fifty eight.

The atomic mass for Cerium is

140.116.

____

Atomic Number

____

Element symbol

____

Element Name

____

Atomic Mass

<u>Praseodymium</u> is a solid.

Name:___________________________________   Date: _____________________

Praseodymium Praseodymium

Praseodymium Praseodymium

Name:_______________________________________ Date: _____________________________

The atomic symbol for

Praseodymium is Pr.

Name:____________________________________ Date:____________________

The atomic number for

Praseodymium is fifty-nine.

Name:___________________________________ Date: _____________________

The atomic mass for

Praseodymium is 140.908.

Atomic Number

Element symbol

Element Name

Atomic Mass

<u>Neodymium</u> comes from the Greek word "neos" (new) & "didymos" (twin).

Name:_______________________________________ Date: _______________________

Neodymium   Neodymium

Neodymium   Neodymium

Name:_______________________________________ Date: _____________________

The atomic symbol for

Neodymium is Nd.

Name:____ Date: _____________________

The atomic number for
Neodymium is sixty.

Name:_________________________________ Date:_________________________

The atomic mass for

Neodymium is 144.240.

____

Atomic Number

____

Element symbol

____

Element Name

____

Atomic Mass

<u>Promethium</u> is named for Prometheus, the Titan, known famously
in Greek mythology.

Name:____ Date: ____________________

The atomic symbol for

Promethium is Pm.

Name:_______________________________ Date:_______________________

The atomic number for

Promethium is sixty one.

The atomic mass for

Promethium is 145.

____
Atomic Number

____
Element symbol

____
Element Name

____
Atomic Mass

<u>Samarium</u> will ignite in air at about 150 °C.

Name:____ Date: ___________________

The atomic symbol for

Samarium is Sm.

The atomic number for
Samarium is sixty two.

The atomic mass for Samarium is 150.36.

____
Atomic Number

____
Element symbol

____
Element Name

____
Atomic Mass

Name:_______________________________ Date:_______________________

Europium Europium Europium

Europium

The atomic symbol for
Europium is Eu.

The atomic number for

Europium is sixty three.

Name:_________________________________ Date: _______________________

The atomic mass for Europium

is 151.964.

315

____
Atomic Number

____
Element symbol

____
Element Name

____
Atomic Mass

<u>Gadolinium</u> has a silvery-white appearance.

Name: _______________________________________ Date: _______________________

Gadolinium   Gadolinium

Gadolinium   Gadolinium

Name:____ Date: ____________________

The atomic symbol for

Gadolinium is Gd.

Name:____ Date: ____________________

The atomic number for

Gadolinium is sixty four.

The atomic mass for

Gadolinium is 157.25.

FILL IN THE BLANKS BELOW WITH THE CORRECT INFORMATION

320

____

Atomic Number

____

Element symbol

____

Element Name

____

Atomic Mass

<u>Terbium</u> is a silvery, soft, ductile, & malleable, rare earth metal.

Name:____ Date:____________________________

Terbium   Terbium   Terbium

Terbium

Name:_________________________________ Date: _______________________

The atomic symbol for

Terbiu is Tb.

Name:____ Date:______________________________

The atomic number for

Terbiu is sixty-five.

Name:_________________________________ Date: _____________________

The atomic mass for Terbiu is

158.925.

FILL IN THE BLANKS BELOW WITH THE CORRECT INFORMATION

____
Atomic Number

____
Element symbol

____
Element Name

____
Atomic Mass

<u>Dysprosium</u> is not found free in nature but rather in several minerals.

Name: _______________________________ Date: _______________________

Name:____ Date:_____________________

The atomic symbol for

Dysprosium is Dy.

The atomic number for
Dysprosium is sixty-six.

Name:_______________________________________ Date: _____________________

The atomic mass for

Dysprosium is 162.5.

330

____

Atomic Number

____

Element symbol

____

Element Name

____

Atomic Mass

<u>Holmium</u> has unusual magnetic properties.

Name: ___________________________ Date: ___________________

Holmium   Holmium   Holmium

Holmium

Name:_________________________________ Date: _________________

The atomic symbol for

Holmium is Ho.

Name:____ Date:_____________________

The atomic number for

Holmium is sixty seven.

The atomic mass for Holmium is 164.93.

____
Atomic Number

____
Element symbol

____
Element Name

____
Atomic Mass

<u>Erbium</u> glows bright pink under fluorescent light.

Name: _______________________________   Date: _______________________

Erbium   Erbium   Erbium   Erbium

Name:____ Date: ____________________

The atomic symbol for Ebrium

is Er.

Name:____ Date: _________________________

The atomic number for Ebrium

is sixty eight.

The atomic mass for Ebrium is 167.259.

____
Atomic Number

____
Element symbol

____
Element Name

____
Atomic Mass

Name:_______________________________   Date: _______________________

Thulium   Thulium   Thulium

Thulium

Name:_________________________________ Date:_________________

The atomic number for Thulium

sixty nine.

Name:_________________________________ Date: _____________________

The atomic mass for Thulium is

168.937.

345

____

Atomic Number

____

Element symbol

____

Element Name

____

Atomic Mass

<u>Ytterbium</u> has the lowest boiling point of the rare earth metals.

Name:____ Date: _______________________

Ytterbium Ytterbium Ytterbium

Ytterbium

Name:_________________________________ Date:_____________________

The atomic symbol for

Ytterbium is Yb.

The atomic number for

Ytterbium is seventy.

The atomic mass for Ytterbium is 173.04.

350

Atomic Number

Element symbol

Element Name

Atomic Mass

<u>Lutetium</u> was originally named lutecium until 1949.

Name:_______________________________________ Date:___________________________

Lutetium   Lutetium   Lutetium

Lutetium

Name:_________________________________ Date: _______________________

The atomic symbol for

Lutetium is Lu.

Name:____ Date: _____________________

The atomic number for

Lutetium is sevety one.

353

Name:____ Date: _________________________

The atomic mass for Lutetium
is 174.967.

____

Atomic Number

____

Element symbol

____

Element Name

____

Atomic Mass

A sample of <u>Hafnium</u> can spontaneously combust in air.

Name:____ Date: ___________________

Hafnium   Hafnium   Hafnium

Hafnium

The atomic symbol for

Hafnium is Hf.

Name:____ Date: _______________________

The atomic number for

Hafnium is seventy two.

Name:_______________________________________ Date: _______________________________

The atomic mass for Hafnium

is 178.49.

Atomic Number

Element symbol

Element Name

Atomic Mass

<u>Tantalum</u> was discovered in 1802.

Name:____ Date:_____________________________

Tantalum   Tantalum   Tantalum

Tantalum

The atomic symbol for

Tantalum is Ta.

Name:__________________________________ Date: ___________________

The atomic number for

Tantalum is sevety three.

The atomic mass for Tantalum
is 180.948.

____

Atomic Number

____

Element symbol

____

Element Name

____

Atomic Mass

Tungsten has the highest melting point of all metals.

Name: ____ Date: _______________________

Tungsten   Tungsten   Tungsten

Tungsten

Name:____ Date:_____________________

The atomic symbol for

Tungsten is W.

Name:_________________________________ Date: _______________

The atomic number for

Tungsten is seventy four.

Name:_______________________________________ Date:___________________________

The atomic mass for Tungsten
is 183.84.

Atomic Number

Element symbol

Element Name

Atomic Mass

<u>Rhenium</u> was named after the River Rhine in Germany.

Name:_________________________________ Date: ___________________

Rhenium   Rhenium   Rhenium

Rhenium

Name:___________________________________ Date: __________________________

The atomic symbol for

Rhenium is Re.

Name:_________________________________ Date:_________________________

The atomic number for

Rhenium is seventy-five.

Name:_________________________________ Date: _____________________

The atomic mass for Rhenium is 186.20.

FILL IN THE BLANKS BELOW WITH THE CORRECT INFORMATION

____

Atomic Number

____

Element symbol

____

Element Name

____

Atomic Mass

<u>Osmium</u> is twice as dense as Lead.

Name:_________________________________ Date:_______________________

Osmium   Osmium   Osmium

Osmium

Name:_________________________________ Date: _______________________

The atomic symbol for

Osmium is Os.

Name:____ Date: ___________________

The atomic number for

Osmium is seventy six.

The atomic mass for Osmium
is 190.23.

____

Atomic Number

____

Element symbol

____

Element Name

____

Atomic Mass

<u>Iridium</u> is the most corrosion-resistant metal known to man.

Name:_______________________________________ Date: _______________________

Name:___________________________________ Date: _____________________

The atomic symbol for

Iridium is Ir.

The atomic number for Iridium is seventy seven

Name:____ Date: ___________________

The atomic mass for Iridium is

192.217.

Atomic Number

Element symbol

Element Name

Atomic Mass

Name:____   Date:___________________________

Platinum   Platinum   Platinum

Platinum

Name:____ Date: ____________________________

The atomic symbol for

Platinum is Pt.

The atomic number for

Platinum is seventy eight.

Name:____ Date:___________________________

The atomic mass for Platinum

is 195.078.

____
Atomic Number

____
Element symbol

____
Element Name

____
Atomic Mass

Oceans are the greatest single reservoir of <u>Gold.</u>

Name:_________________________________   Date: _______________________

Gold   Gold   Gold   Gold

Name:_________________________________ Date: _____________________

The atomic symbol for Gold is

Au.

The atomic number for Gold is seventy nine.

Name:_________________________________ Date: _____________________

The atomic mass for Gold is

196.967.

Atomic Number

Element symbol

Element Name

Atomic Mass

<u>Mercury</u> can be extremely poisonous to humans.

Name:_______________________________ Date: _______________________

Mercury   Mercury   Mercury

Mercury

Name:____ Date:____________________________

The atomic symbol for Mercury

is Hg.

Name:___________________________________ Date: _______________________

The atomic number for Mercury

is eighty.

Name:____ Date:_____________________________

The atomic mass for Mercury is

200.59.

____

Atomic Number

____

Element symbol

____

Element Name

____

Atomic Mass

Most <u>Thallium</u> is used by the electronics industry in photoelectric cells.

Name:_________________________________ Date: _____________________

Thallium   Thallium   Thallium

Thallium

Name:_______________________________________ Date: ___________________________

The atomic symbol for

Thallium is Tl.

Name:_________________________________ Date: _______________________

The atomic number for

Thallium is eighty-one.

Name:________________________________ Date: _____________________

The atomic masss for Thallium is 204.383.

____

Atomic Number

____

Element symbol

____

Element Name

____

Atomic Mass

<u>Lead</u> is a metallic gray, solid at room temperature, it gives off a high-pitched "scream" when bent.

Name: _______________________________________ Date: _______________________

Lead   Lead   Lead   Lead

Name:_____________________________________ Date: ____________________

The atomic symbol for Lead is

Pb.

Name:_______________________________ Date: _______________________

The atomic number for Lead is
eighty two.

The atomic mass for Lead is

207.2.

Atomic Number

Element symbol

Element Name

Atomic Mass

<u>Bismuth</u> is denser as a liquid than as a solid.

Name:_______________________________________ Date: _______________________

Bismuth Bismuth Bismuth

Bismuth

The atomic symbol for

Bismuth is Bi.

The atomic number for

Bismuth is eighty three.

Name:_______________________________________ Date: _______________________

The atomic mass for Bismuth is
208.98.

____

Atomic Number

____

Element symbol

____

Element Name

____

Atomic Mass

Name:_______________________________________   Date: _______________________

Polonium   Polonium   Polonium

Polonium

Name:____ Date: _______________________

The atomic symbol for

Polonium is Po.

The atomic number for
Polonium is eighty four.

Name:__________________________________ Date: __________________________

The atomic mass for Polonium

is 209.

____

Atomic Number

____

Element symbol

____

Element Name

____

Atomic Mass

<u>Astatine</u> only has one atom.

Name:_________________________________ Date: _____________________

Astatine   Astatine   Astatine

Astatine

The atomic symbol for Astatine is At.

Name:_______________________________________ Date: ___________________________

The atomic number for Astatine

is eighty five.

Name:_________________________________ Date: _____________________

The atomic mass for Astatine

is 210.

FILL IN THE BLANKS BELOW WITH THE CORRECT INFORMATION

425

____

Atomic Number

Element symbol

Element Name

Atomic Mass

<u>Radon</u> is oderless.

Name:_______________________________________ Date:_________________________

Name:_________________________________ Date: _______________________

The atomic symbol for Radon

is Rn.

Name: _______________________ Date: _______________________
The atomic number for Radon is eighty six.

Name:_________________________________ Date:___________________

The atomic mass for Radon is

222.

Atomic Number

Element symbol

Element Name

Atomic Mass

The melting point of <u>Francium</u> is 27 °C.

Name:_____________________________________   Date: _____________________

Francium Francium Francium

Francium

Name:_______________________________ Date: _______________________

The atomic symbol for

Francium is Fr.

Name:____________________________________ Date:__________________________

The atomic number for

Francium is eighty seven.

The atomic mass for Francium

is 223.

435

____

Atomic Number

____

Element symbol

____

Element Name

____

Atomic Mass

Marie and Pierre Currie discovered <u>Radium</u> in 1898.

Name:_____________________________________ Date:_____________________

Radium   Radium   Radium

Radium

The atomic symbol for

Radium is Ra.

Name:_________________________________ Date: _______________________

The atomic number for

Radium is eighty eight.

The atomic mass for Radium is

226.

____

Atomic Number

____

Element symbol

____

Element Name

____

Atomic Mass

The word <u>Actinium</u> comes from the Greek word "aktis or aktinos," which means "beam or ray."

Name:_______________________________________ Date: _____________________

Actinium   Actinium   Actinium

Actinium

Name:________________________________ Date: ____________________

The atomic symbol for

Actinium is Ac.

Name:_______________________________________ Date: _______________________

The atomic number for

Actinium is eighty-nine.

The atomic mass for Actinium is 227.

____

Atomic Number

____

Element symbol

____

Element Name

____

Atomic Mass

<u>Thorium</u> is named for Thor, the ancient Norse god of thunder.

Name: _______________________________   Date: _______________________

Thorium   Thorium   Thorium

Thorium

Name:_________________________________ Date:_______________________

The atomic symbol for Thorium
is Th.

Name:________________________________ Date:________________

The atomic number for Thorium is ninety.

Name:_________________________________ Date:_______________________

The atomic mass for Thorium

is 232.0381.

____
Atomic Number

____
Element symbol

____
Element Name

____
Atomic Mass

<u>Protactinium</u> has no stable isotopes.

Name:______________________________   Date:__________________

Protactinium   Protactinium

Protactinium   Protactinium

Name:_________________________________ Date:_______________________

The atomic symbol for

Protactinium is Pa.

Name:____ Date:___________________________

The atomic number for

Protactinium is ninety one.

Name:____ Date: _______________________

The atomic mass for

Protactinium is 231.0359.

455

____

Atomic Number

____

Element symbol

____

Element Name

____

Atomic Mass

<u>Uranium</u> has a melting point of about 3,818 °C (about 6,904 °F).

Name:_______________________________________ Date: ___________________

Uranium   Uranium   Uranium

Uranium

Name:____ Date:_____________________________

The atomic symbol for
Uranium is U.

Name:_______________________________________ Date:_____________________

The atomic number for

Uranium is ninety two.

Name:________________________________ Date: ___________________

The atomic mass for uranium

is 238.0289.

____

Atomic Number

____

Element symbol

____

Element Name

____

Atomic Mass

<u>Neptunium</u> was discovered in 1940 by Edwin McMillan & Philip H. Ableson.

Name:____ Date: ___________________________

Neptunium   Neptunium

Neptunium   Neptunium

The atomic symbol for

Neptunium is Np.

Name:_______________________________________ Date: _______________________

The atomic number for

Neptunium is ninety three.

Name:_________________________________ Date:_______________________

The atomic mass for

Neptunium is 237.

465

____

Atomic Number

____

Element symbol

____

Element Name

____

Atomic Mass

<u>Plutonium</u> is named for the dwarf planet Pluto.

Name:_______________________________________   Date: ____________________

The atomic symbol for

Plutonium is Pu.

The atomic number for
Plutonium is ninety four.

Name:_________________________________ Date: _______________________

The atomic mass for Plutonium

is 244.

____
Atomic Number

____
Element symbol

____
Element Name

____
Atomic Mass

<u>Americium</u> was first produced in 1944 during the Manhattan Project.

Name:____ Date:___________________________

Americium   Americium

Americium   Americium

Name:_______________________________________ Date: _____________________

The atomic symbol for

Americium is Am.

The atomic number for Americium is ninety five.

The atomic mass for

Americium is 243.

475

____

Atomic Number

____

Element symbol

____

Element Name

____

Atomic Mass

<u>Curium</u> is named after chemist & physicist Marie Curie & her husband, Pierre Curie.

Name:_________________________________ Date: _______________________

Curium Curium Curium Curium

Name:_______________________________________ Date: _____________________

The atomic symbol for Curium

is Cm.

Name:_______________________________________ Date: _____________________

The atomic number for Curium

is ninety six.

The atomic mass for Curium is 247.

Atomic Number

Element symbol

Element Name

Atomic Mass

<u>Berkelium</u> is an artificially produced element.

Name:_________________________________ Date: _______________________

Berkelium Berkelium Berkelium

Berkelium

Name:______________________________ Date: __________________

The atomic symbol for

Berkelium is Bk.

Name:____ Date: _______________________

The atomic number for

Berkelium is ninety-seven.

Name:____ Date: _______________________

The atomic mass for Berkelium is 247.

____

Atomic Number

____

Element symbol

____

Element Name

____

Atomic Mass

<u>Californium</u> is malleable and so soft it can be sliced with a razor blade.

Name:_______________________________________ Date: _______________________

The atomic symbol for

Californium is Cf.

Name:_______________________________________ Date: _______________________

The atomic number for

Californium is ninety eight.

Name:____ Date: _____________________

The atomic mass for

Californium is 251.

489

____

Atomic Number

____

Element symbol

____

Element Name

____

Atomic Mass

<u>Einsteinium</u> is highly radioactive & glows with a blue light.

Name:________________________________ Date: _______________________

Name:_________________________________ Date: _______________________

The atomic symbol for

Einsteinium is Es.

Name:_______________________________________ Date: ___________________________

The atomic number for

Einsteinium is ninety nine.

Name:_____________________________________ Date: _____________________

The atomic mass for

Einsteinium is 252.

495

____

Atomic Number

____

Element symbol

____

Element Name

____

Atomic Mass

<u>Fermium</u> is named for the physicist Enrico Fermi.

Name:_________________________________ Date: _______________________

Fermium   Fermium   Fermium

Fermium

The atomic symbol for

Fermium is Fm.

Name:_________________________________ Date: _________________

The atomic number for

Fermium is one hundred.

Name:_______________________________________ Date:_____________________

The atomic mass for Fermium

is 257.

FILL IN THE BLANKS BELOW WITH THE CORRECT INFORMATION

____

Atomic Number

____

Element symbol

____

Element Name

____

Atomic Mass

<u>Mendelevium</u> was first created on February 19, 1955.

Name:_________________________________ Date:_______________________

Mendelevium   Mendelevium

Mendelevium   Mendelevium

Name:_________________________________ Date: _______________________

The atomic symbol for

Mendelevium is Md.

The atomic number for Mendelevium is one hundred one.

Name:_________________________________ Date:_________________________

The atomic mass for

Mendelevium is 258.

____
Atomic Number

____
Element symbol

____
Element Name

____
Atomic Mass

The creation of <u>Nobelium</u> was announced in 1958.

Name:_______________________________________ Date: _______________________

Nobelium   Nobelium   Nobelium

Nobelium

The atomic symbol for

Nobelium is No.

The atomic number for

Nobelium is one hundred two.

Name:_________________________________ Date: _____________________

The atomic mass for

Nobelium is 259.

510

____

Atomic Number

____

Element symbol

____

Element Name

____

Atomic Mass

<u>Lawrencium</u> is named for physicist Ernest O. Lawrence.

Name:_______________________________________ Date: _____________________________

Lawrencium   Lawrencium

Lawrencium   Lawrencium

The atomic symbolfor
Lawrencium is Lr.

Name:____ Date: _____________________

The atomic number for

Lawrencium is one hundred

three.

Name:_________________________________ Date: _________________________

The atomic mass for

Lawrencium is 262.

____

Atomic Number

____

Element symbol

____

Element Name

____

Atomic Mass

<u>Rutherfordium</u> was added by the International Unions of Pure & Applied Chemistry as an element in 1992.

Name:____   Date: ____________________

The atomic symbol for

Rutherfordium is Rf.

Name:_______________________________ Date: ___________________

The atomic number for

Rutherfordium is one hundred

four.

Name:_______________________________________ Date: ___________________

The atomic mass for

Rutherfordium is 261.

520

____
Atomic Number

____
Element symbol

____
Element Name

____
Atomic Mass

Name:____ Date: ______________________

Dubnium   Dubnium   Dubnium

Dubnium

Name:_________________________________ Date: ___________________

The atomic symbol for

Dubnium is Db.

Name:______________________________________ Date:______________________

The atomic number for

Dubnium is one hundred five.

The atomic mass for Dubnium

is 262.

525

____

Atomic Number

____

Element symbol

____

Element Name

____

Atomic Mass

<u>Seaborgium</u> is the first element named after a living person.

Name:___________________________________ Date: ___________________

Seaborgium   Seaborgium

Seaborgium   Seaborgium

Name:____ Date: _____________________________

The atomic symbol for

Seaborgium is Sg.

The atomic number for

Seaborgium is one hundred six.

The atomic mass for

Seaborgium is 266.

530

____

Atomic Number

____

Element symbol

____

Element Name

____

Atomic Mass

Named for a Nobel Prize winner, <u>Bohrium</u>, belongs in Group 7 of the Periodic Table.

Name:____ Date:_____________________________

Bohrium   Bohrium   Bohrium

Bohrium

Name:_________________________________ Date: _______________________

The atomic symbol for

Bohrium is Bh.

Name:___________________________________ Date:____________________________

The atomic number for

Bohrium is one hundred seven.

Name:____ Date: _____________________

The atomic mass for Bohrium is 264.

____

Atomic Number

____

Element symbol

____

Element Name

____

Atomic Mass

<u>Hassium</u> has 108 protons present in its nucleus.

Name: _______________________________ Date: _______________________

Hassium   Hassium   Hassium

Hassium

Name:____ Date: _____________________

The atomic symbol for

Hassium is Hs.

Name:____ Date: _______________________

The atomic number for

Hassium is one hundred eight.

Name:____ Date: _____________________

The atomic mass for Hassium

is 277.

Atomic Number

Element symbol

Element Name

Atomic Mass

<u>Meitnerium</u> is named after a woman scientist, Lise Meitner, who co-discovered the process of nuclear fission.

Name: _______________________________   Date: _______________________

The atomic symbol for

Meitnerium is Mt.

Name:____ Date:_____________________

The atomic number for

Meitnerium is one hundred nine.

Name:____ Date: ___________________

The atomic mass for

Meitnerium is 268.

545

____
Atomic Number

____
Element symbol

____
Element Name

____
Atomic Mass

<u>**Darmstadtium**</u> **is a synthetic chemical that was discovered in 1994.**

Name:____ Date: _______________________

Darmstadtium   Darmstadtium

Darmstadtium   Darmstadtium

Name:_________________________________ Date: _____________________

The atomic symbol for

Darmstadtium is Ds.

Name:_______________________________________ Date: _______________________

The atomic number for

Darmstadtium is one hundred

ten.

The atomic mass for

Darmstadtium is 281.

550

____
Atomic Number

____
Element symbol

____
Element Name

____
Atomic Mass

<u>Roentgenium</u> is a man-made radioactive element & is not found in any natural environment on Earth.

Name:_______________________________ Date:_______________________

Roentgenium Roentgenium

Roentgenium Roentgenium

The atomic symbol for
Roentgenium is Rg.

The atomic number for Roentgenium is one hundred eleven.

Name:____ Date: _____________________

The atomic mass for

Roentgenium is 272.

FILL IN THE BLANKS BELOW WITH THE CORRECT INFORMATION

Atomic Number

Element symbol

Element Name

Atomic Mass

<u>Copernicium</u> is named after the astronomer Nicolaus Copernicus.

Name:_________________________________ Date: _____________________

Name:_______________________________________ Date:_____________________

The atomic symbol for

Copernicium is Cn.

Name:_______________________________________ Date:_____________________

The atomic number for Copernicium is one hundred twelve.

Name:_______________________________ Date:_______________________

560

____

Atomic Number

____

Element symbol

____

Element Name

____

Atomic Mass

<u>Nihonium</u> is toxic due to its radioactivity.

Name:____ Date:_____________________________

Nihonium Nihonium Nihonium

Nihonium

The atomic symbol for

Nihonium is Nh.

Name:____ Date:____________________

The atomic number for

Nihonium is one hundred

thirteen.

Name:_________________________________ Date: _______________________

The atomic mass for Nihonium

is 286.

____

Atomic Number

____

Element symbol

____

Element Name

____

Atomic Mass

<u>Flerovium</u> was first discovered in Russia in 1998.

Name:____   Date: _______________________

Flerovium Flerovium Flerovium

Flerovium

Name:_________________________________ Date:_____________________

The atomic symbol for

Flerovium is Fl.

The atomic number for
Flerovium is one hundred
fourteen.

Name:____ Date: ______________________

The atomic mass for Flerovium

is 289.

____
Atomic Number

____
Element symbol

____
Element Name

____
Atomic Mass

<u>Moscovium</u> is also known as Ununpentium.

Name:____ Date: ____________________

Moscovium   Moscovium

Moscovium   Moscovium

Name:_______________________________ Date: _______________________

The atomic symbol for

Moscovium is Mc.

Name:_______________________________________ Date: _____________________________

The atomic number for

Moscovium is one hundred

fifteen.

Name:____ Date:____________________________

The atomic mass for

Moscovium is 289.

575

____
Atomic Number

____
Element symbol

____
Element Name

____
Atomic Mass

<u>Livermorium</u> is expected to be solid at room temperature.

Name: _______________________________ Date: _______________________

Livermorium   Livermorium

Livermorium   Livermorium

Name:_____________________________________ Date: _____________________

The atomic symbol for

Livermorium is Lv.

Name:____ Date: _____________________

The atomic number for

Livermorium is one hundred

sixteen.

Name:_________________________________ Date: _________________________

The atomic mass for

Livermorium is 293.

____
Atomic Number

____
Element symbol

____
Element Name

____
Atomic Mass

<u>Tennessine</u> is also known as Ununseptium.

Name:____ Date: _______________________

The atomic symbol for
Tennessine is Ts.

Name:_________________________________ Date:_______________________

The atomic number for

Tennessine is one hundred

seventeen.

Name:_________________________________ Date: _____________________

The atomic mass for

Tennessine is 294.

585

____
Atomic Number

____
Element symbol

____
Element Name

____
Atomic Mass

Name: _______________________________________   _______________________________

Name: ________________________________   ________________________________

The atomic symbol for

Oganesson is Og.

Name: _______________________________   _______________________________

The atomic number for

Oganesson is one hundred

eighteen.

Name: _______________________________   _______________________

The atomic mass for

Oganesson is 294.

Atomic Number

Element symbol

Element Name

Atomic Mass